THE FLEECE ERA

THE FLEECE ERA

JOANNA LILLEY

BRICK BOOKS

Library and Archives Canada Cataloguing in Publication

Lilley, Joanna, 1967-, author
  The fleece era / Joanna Lilley.

Poems.
ISBN 978-1-926829-89-0 (pbk.)

  I. Title.

PS8623.I43F54 2014   C811'.6   C2013-907314-0

We acknowledge the Canada Council for the Arts, the Government of
Canada through the Canada Book Fund, and the Ontario Arts Council
for their support of our publishing program.

The author photo was taken by Marten Berkman.

This book is set in ITC New Baskerville.

Design and layout by Cheryl Dipede.
Printed and bound by Sunville Printco Inc.

Brick Books
431 Boler Road, Box 20081
London, Ontario N6K 4G6
www.brickbooks.ca

For Glenn, the music to my words

CONTENTS

A RIDDLE

Overheard — 3
The Middle of Nowhere — 4
At the Post Office — 5
Stroke — 6
Through Heathrow, Terminal Three — 7
The Collection — 8
Aunt — 10
Lady of Gifts — 11
Counting — 13
If I Had Children — 14
Sweet Tooth — 15
Unfinished — 16
Edinburgh — 17
Farmer Ants — 18
Paper Trail — 20
Semi-detached — 22
We Can Be Anything — 24

EMOTIONAL EXPENDITURE

The Churches Are Full of Men — 31
Inside — 32
Liz's New Painting — 34
Band — 36
Ugly — 37
We Don't Hate Her — 38
Notes at a Concert — 39
Lucky — 40
The Piano Tuner — 42
Parhelion — 43
St. Maarten — 44
Unravelled — 46
Work-Life Balance — 48
At Work — 49
Peterhead, Aberdeenshire — 50

At Sea 63

At Sea 64
Recovery Point 65
Touching My Husband 66
Vancouver Heart 67

NOBODY ELSE DIES

Walking in the English Countryside on a Sunny Day 71
Biology Lesson 73
White Dog 75
Keeping Warm in Antarctica 77
Year of the Sheep 78
Red Canoe 80
Salt Flats 82
Fish Lake Ridge 83
The Names of Things 84
Stone 86
Earth Crack 87
Cat and Mouse 88
Ten Thousand Trees 89
The Fleece Era 91
This Is the House 92
Mountain Time 93
Ediphile 95
Landowner 96
Neo-colonialist 97
You were probably genetically programmed 98
Earth Twin 100

ACKNOWLEDGEMENTS
103

ABOUT THE AUTHOR
105

A RIDDLE

OVERHEARD

I never hang up first, always wait
for the tremble in my mother's hand
not replacing the receiver properly
beside her saucer of custard creams,
and I continue to receive:
she'll see sense, she'll come back.
I shouted once, I won't!
my small voice scrambled by her hearing aids,
tinny as if I were a cookie crumb
balancing on the rim,
shouting from the shore
of my mother's Atlantic teacup.

THE MIDDLE OF NOWHERE

My family won't visit this
faraway place of half-year
winters, centuries of quiet,
where aspen shadows dress
the snow in long blue ribbons.

My family says I've run away
from life, couldn't cope with
being in the thick of it any more.
How do they know
where is the thick, the thin?

Here, between the silent aspens,
is the thick of it.
Spliced by sisters,
pinched between parents:
there's the thin.

AT THE POST OFFICE

...my father's
heart pushes him downstairs again,
I won't be able to get back to England.

I'm too old to hear high-pitched
sounds any more, but the drone
of danger has got so loud
I might as well live
next to the airport.

Leaving the post office,
I bend to a tub of pansies
on the sidewalk and sniff
the blood-thin petals
already covered in ice crystals.

STROKE

For the last twenty years
my mother has sat shedding
skin cells for someone else
to vacuum, while she tears people

out of magazines, slides them
into plastic sleeves. She thinks
they're her children but usually
they're people everyone knows.

In my dreams, she rips clouds,
drops pieces to the ground.
In my father's dreams, she talks;
he never tells me what she says.

I stayed late at work again today,
eyes shut, to hear the vacuuming:
it was the only way
my mother could ever wake me.

THROUGH HEATHROW, TERMINAL THREE

makes her so sleepy, she tucks
the pebbles under her tongue.
On the Tube, her purse and coat float,
her suitcase thuds, heavy even without
maple fudge for her mother.

On the street, round the corner,
she coughs the pebbles out,
kicks them through the bars of a sewer grate.
She's nearly at the house
with the sash window weights
that pull at her eyelids.

She'll smile with her eyes open,
sleep until it feels like yesterday.
She'll say she's sorry by painting
the kitchen and ringing the plumber.
Then she'll give her father
the watercolour lesson she's been
promising for nearly twenty years.

THE COLLECTION

Her birthday was yesterday
but she's still waiting for the mail.
She picks up the chunk of translucent calcite
her son gave her last year, puts it down again.

She finds a piece of paper and a pencil
and draws a line. Holding the rock
to the window, she places the paper behind.
The line is doubled; calcite splits light.

A gap year, her son calls it.
He's flown over water she can't cross
because that would be meeting
his father more than halfway.

As soon as he could walk, her son,
worming fingers into the dirt,
swayed to her with a pebble of granite.
He's given her a rock for her birthday

ever since. She doesn't put them with her
own father's collection in the cabinet
she ran to each time her parents argued,
picking up each specimen to check

the lightest, shiniest, prettiest.
When her father left, she smashed
an orb of soapstone with his rock
hammer to see what was inside.

smooth a..
Her son's letter says *come visit.*
If she throws all her rocks into the ocean,
there might be enough for a bridge.

AUNT

I stand in late light
at my nephew's attic window
as he sleeps. Below,
his mother weeps.
I leak the powerlessness of aunts.
I can't fling words far enough
for a sister to catch.
Even easy ones:
he's not coming back.
I'm going to chuck what I have left
out the window, go home
and start a college fund.
Abstract nouns tap like rain.
Proper nouns thwack like hail.
Verbs – wet snow – won't settle.
No more words. No weather.
Only the moon, which
will stay a comma
this entire night.

LADY OF GIFTS

cushion-stuffing hair.

Who would think such
a sweet-looking old lady was
built to withstand earthquakes,
would be the last structure standing

when my parents collapsed
from the punch of having too
many children who wouldn't
do as they were told.

She gave my father kunzite
so he could breathe.
A pink crystal for his pillow
at night, for his handkerchief at day.

For my mother, conversation.
A thin wrist reaching for
a hand in a lap.
Hours and hours

in a sunny front room
across from the cricket ground,
often on only one pot of tea.
For me, home-child, a riddle

she didn't answer before she died:
whether there is more suffering
in having children
than in bearing none.

COUNTING

She knows they never will.
Their father doesn't.

He won't go out in case
they come and he's not there.

Her blood surges, stretching vessels.
She has had a headache for years.

She plucks off healthy leaves,
kicks a bag of compost.

She takes her cigarettes from a pocket,
lights one to dilute the stench of fertile earth.

IF I HAD CHILDREN

If I had children
I would have to stop
reading the book I'm reading
and stop writing the book
I'm writing and stop worrying
about how much sleep
I don't get and I, who cannot listen
to the weather forecast all the way through,
would have to pay attention
for the rest of my life to the rest of theirs.
Every night, I would lay them
under a ceiling and have to remember
to keep them warmer
in winter than in summer.
Every day, I would have to feed them
food that isn't the food
that's killing me. Every night,
I would lay my hand on
their hearts to feel the beat
I take too long to find behind
my own fleshy breast, my wadded ribs.
And eventually I would have to explain
why grown-ups can't sit at the table
politely like children can, why
adults argue, tell each other lies.
Eventually, I would admit
that people firing guns and dropping
bombs do have a choice.
As I was dying, all I would have
to bequeath would be a million pounds
of greenhouse gas emissions.
As I was dying, I'd forget
I'd promised myself never to confess
I nearly didn't have them
because the human race was almost over
and it was clear who was going to win.

SWEET TOOTH

The castle inside
dissolves, unfortified.
I eat it up in wandfuls.

On her bicycle my mother slaloms us
through oaks on the way to the shops.
Sweetness rises, frosts my tongue.
My saliva tastes like sherbet.
In my gut, the first
stalactites of sucrose
begin to grow.

UNFINISHED

I was in the hospital under a week,
no need for a doctor's note at work.
It wasn't a decision I made;
it was started, never completed,

like the sky-blue sweater
my mother tried to knit me.
Up to the waist by my fourteenth
birthday, still armless by Christmas.

Not until my fifteenth year
did my mother admit it wasn't
the job or too much housework
or even the books by her bed,

it was her hands.
I unbuttoned my mother's fingers
from the sweater with a promise
to give it back when she was better.

Once the will was read
and the sweater wasn't in it,
I knew it was my inheritance.
I would learn to knit, finish it,

find a child to put it on.
And I would have done,
if I'd been any good
with my hands.

EDINBURGH

However long I stay,
this won't be me.
I'll always reside
on a half-filled page
of a visitors' book.
The lady sees me
through the watery pane.
Our smiles meet.
Maybe I'll settle
my bill, check out,
rent a basement down a
wrought-iron staircase,
work my way up
to street level.

FARMER ANTS

When white lilies arrive, she goes
around the block,
the wind running after her,
picking up the grief she spills.

When her mother's house is emptied
into her apartment, she goes again,
this time across the country.
She boards whatever's leaving,

leans back to watch as sprockets
pull the land in front of her.
A city of supersized windows
that suck in brackish rain,

slapdash chiselled mountains,
a North Pole of fields,
a black shield of trees.
At another coast the film runs out.

She could have reached back from here
to stop the ventilator, fingers
inside the doctor's hand,
but she stood at her mother's bedside,

the slowest decision she's made,
yet still too quick.
Daughters aren't supposed
to switch off mothers.

She waits in the harbour city for blue
and green to mix with blue and white.
Missing Granville Bridge she walks
Macdonald, water blocking infinity.

...ing Dawn on clotted-blood roses.

Outside, she crouches, peers at a tiny lime
creature making a map from a leaf.
An ant, blackberry-bodied,
nudges the aphid; she's about

to witness murder. But the ant
doesn't. Rather, it touches, tickles,
strokes. It's embarrassing to watch.
Indoors, she Googles ants and aphids.

Ants milk aphids for their sweet
secretions, corral them, farm them, even
rip their wings off so they can never leave.
She once made her mother angel wings,

stuck them to her shoulders
with flour-and-water glue. When they
fell off her mother said it didn't
matter; she didn't want to fly away.

PAPER TRAIL

On her fifth birthday her father folded her inside
an origami house. This, he said through
lambent paper, is how I will protect you.
After a minute for every birthday, he tore her out.
Her sixth birthday, he left her sleeping,
pale potato, until she baked.
The seventh was a screech of tape,
light lines edging waxy planes.
The Japanese, he whispered, live between
paper walls. She read books quickly
but never found anyone hiding in the pages.

Age eight, wallpaper year, he folded
himself beside her, sealing seams
from the inside. Imagine there's been
a gas leak, he said, holding her vellum wrists.
A pair of Anaglypta slippers was her gift.
The next time she heard his fists pressing
creases, she swam into the pocket
on the back of his bedroom door.

She used his lighter to fire the screw of paper
that detonated the recycling bin.
He crouched and she ran, slippers ripping.
Barefoot in the street, marooned
on a warm fish-and-chip wrapper,
she turned the heat of the fiery house
from cheek to cheek. Floating her hand
to the sky, she couldn't see a watermark.
The split of pain was just a paper cut.
She went willingly to the police station,
where she watched hot sheets
become dirtied by printed words.
She wasn't allowed to carry them
to the children's home; she wanted
the paper to cover her face.

Day and year

For their first anniversary,
the one that mattered, her husband made her a kite
of brown bags, bamboo.
He showed her how to poke string
through the middles of paper squares,
see the wind shove them up to kiss the kite.
Messages, he said – airmail – promising
he wouldn't read her flying missives.
But, folded in his arms, she knew he had
when he whispered, it's time to rise
above your past. She let the kite string go,
took the car and drove home almost standing.
A Zippo fuelled and flinted,
she lit the marriage certificate,
a taper to blaze her bridal house.

SEMI-DETACHED

I

His mother took an axe to their home, split it.
Told him the rent from next door
would keep the wolf from their door.
When she caught her cardigan
on the gas stove, she unravelled the lesson.
God-made skin as flammable as man-made fibre.
When his mother wore a fire dress she got greedy.
She whirled upstairs and ate his bed
before the firefighters stopped her dead.

II

The woman who gave him his mother's ashes
asked if he'd be all right, but left
before he knew the answer.
People his mother had ignored in the street
left him casseroles, pasta, muffins and fruit pies
on the overcooked doorstep.
He ate the fruit pies first – he liked the sugar
sprinkled on the top.
The tenants moved out before
he decided if he could ask.
He moved back into the immaculate other side
of his bedroom. He didn't need furniture;
only the certainty of sleeping on unyielding floorboards.

the sweet grit of cleaning his fingernails
with his teeth afterwards.

The cauliflowers, when they came,
were bigger than brains,
the onions loose-skinned,
the turnips hard as winter knees.
The lettuces wore crumpled dresses.
Each carrot was a finger rigid with arthritis.
He waited until night to harvest the crop.
Walking softly, he placed a box
on the doorstep of each house on his street.
He didn't keep anything for himself.
His mother had taught him
how to use the grocery store.

WE CAN BE ANYTHING

Artist

Our mother melts margarine
I'd drink if she wasn't looking.
She adds a crackle of brown sugar,
pours in a long, soft whisper of oats,
salted by slim fingers I wish I'd inherited.
We're making flapjack.
We're laying a trap.
When flapjack has cooled as long
as it cooked, it's perfect.
Eldest of four disordered sisters,
an octave older than me,
you know this too.

Our mother lays a tea towel
over the flapjack
like a blanket over you
and takes me swimming.
Returning, she lifts the tea towel,
self-taught magician,
to reveal a silver square,
a diminishing daughter with at least
a little food in her stomach.

Your lines are sharper than you
can draw, your stomach scraped
deeper than you can sculpt.
At night I dream you bind my hands
in gauze and plaster until
they're voluptuous. Mine
are forgeries of yours:
large-knuckled, double-jointed thumbs.
You've forgotten your own hands;
the wire is showing through.

You shrink-wrap your hips,
choreograph yourself
into a small sweaty space.

Another tray of flapjack left to cool
for that other sister,
you say it was our springing
dog who licked it silver-clean.
You're better at mathematics than me.
I never put two and two together
until you deliver a bile-scented letter
to the kitchen table confessing
it wasn't the dog, nor were
the Easter eggs or bread.

Clasping a prayer of tea
to cram your stomach,
you kneel at the pantry door,
begging us to keep it locked.
Our parents take you everywhere they can,
tell everyone who thinks they know
why you can't stop eating.
Patient faces talk to you in small rooms
and to us in corridors. When you ask,
we unlock you,
telling you lies we mean.

In a city by a sea,
other arms pull you up for air,
resuscitate you with religion.
You give up the barre
our father built for an endless past
you can spend the rest of your lives
remembering.

Musician

We raise our hands out of the sea,
pour back sun-sparkled gems.
We've always found it easy to be sisters.
I drip onto a swelling notebook
while you practise your embouchure
until, bored with our Ionian paradise,
we board another train.

You pick carefully from the palette
our parents gave us all to share.
We can be anything
as long as we're artists.
If you can draw or dance,
we'll never know,
but you play sweetly enough
to make us cry, though
colleges don't care for tears.
Keeping your mouth full
keeps your mind off music.

Our mother screams that you've both
been brainwashed. Our father
grabs and drops the phone.
I should have known you'd
pass your religion on to me.
If I hadn't taken it,
my hands would have been free
to break our mother's fall.

Writer

Growing not up but sideways,
I dodge the butts of your palms.
Youngest and smallest,
I daren't grow higher than any of you.
Largest and shortest,
I eat as much as I can stomach.
A tuberous, underground person
who burrowed so deep
I came up in another land.

Brother

You were a white-bread brother
in a brown-bread house.
Last time I saw our mother
the photograph was still
on her chest of drawers, faded
from black and white to grey and blue.
Your fingers, sea anemones
on the keyboard.
Blond, aged ten,
winning a piano competition.
Of all of us, you have
our mother's hands.
You stopped playing after you
fixed your first bicycle chain
and oil-mapped the ridges, lakes
and valleys of your fingerprints.

Yesterday, you told me on the phone,
you made our mother flapjack
because you're the only one there.
When it came out too crumbly,
you put it back into the pan
and added treacle.
You only gave it to our mother
when it was perfect.

EMOTIONAL EXPENDITURE

THE CHURCHES ARE FULL OF MEN

~~...es are full of children.~~

My parents are full of dying.

My husband is full of the futility of trying.

The books on my shelves are full of words

that I spend my days rearranging.

I used to look up words I didn't understand.

Now, I prefer not knowing what they mean.

INSIDE

He knows his way around your body
better than you do.
After a snooze in your spleen, he tickles
your hippocampus with white hairs
he plucked from your mother's head
the last time you kissed her.
He slides down your intestines
as you sleep, lands in your bladder
so you have to get up to sit on the loo
at three, his happy hour.
At dawn he paints your throat
with dissatisfaction so when you wake up
you can't say anything nice.

At work, when you're at your desk too long,
he twangs your tendons until you
go looking for gossip.
When you sit back down he stands
on the floor of your lungs
and blows until you sigh
and wonder why you took this job.

Afternoons, he loves to wear
a thick coat of chocolate,
watch a wave of theobromine
push out your artery walls
and suck a rip current through your heart.

...ging your unfulfilled potential.
It's the orifice your sister warned you about
whenever you both lay on grass,
except she only told you
spiders would get in.

LIZ'S NEW PAINTING

Liz shows me her new painting.
It's in her dining room.
A sturdy rounded woman,
nearly as fat as me, kneeling

with a smooth plump cat
curved in her arms.
A Sandra Bierman, I say.
Liz is surprised I know.

It's wrong, she says,
not looking at my belly,
the pressure on women
to be thin. She smiles and adds,

What I like about Bierman
is she shows how nurturing,
earthy, women are,
how grounded.

I don't tell her she forgot jolly.
I could play the xylophone
on Liz's ribs,
the drums on her stomach.

I want to hook my fingers
under her clavicles,
hang her in a tree until
she tinkles like a wind chime.

looked at myself in a mirror

for twenty years?
Did you know
I eat all my meals
with my eyes closed?

BAND

The strumming mother is not quite
as tiresome as her droning daughter.
I wish they'd get their knees dirty
and weed this bluegrass song.
I want to forget sitting on a plastic
chair in an overheated Legion hall.
I don't want to be reminded youth
isn't everything or to speculate
whether the blood on the wall
in the ladies' loo is menstrual
or the yawn-swipe of some
other listener who bit
through her lip to stay awake,
blood always being a good excuse
for a woman to leave.

UGLY

...ter's steel-wool scrub.
I've been at it all day,
even in meetings, rubbing
my chin with the pillow
of my thumb to rasp a stout hair
I knew was black.
I pinch it now with tweezers.
I should try herbicide
on my forty-fuzz.
It's time for that
chin Brazilian.

WE DON'T HATE HER

She laughs as if she's
ringing a bell for service.
Her words are as plucked
as her eyebrows.
She can wear white
even when she's pregnant.
Especially when she is pregnant.
She buttons her cardigan only
at the neck, so her pink-sweatered
baby bump is a rosebud.
Ten years before she found
the father, she named the daughter
that she knew she'd one day have.
It was so long before the baby
showed, we thought she'd got it
wrong, but she knew it was safe
to tell us early. Pregnancy
is easy. She wonders
what all the fuss is about.
Childbirth will be easy too.
Her daughter will be clever,
pretty, slim; she'll never break
her mother's heart.

NOTES AT A CONCERT

The guitarist's mouth is easy-smile.
His stomach swells below his black roll-neck:
good wine, seafood, the occasional
game of squash. He's San Francisco.
His slapping hands
look as soft as a solicitor's,
but there must be calluses.
The double bass player's fingers are thick sticks,
his forehead broad. His lips curl
towards his nostrils; he's Rossetti's Beatrice –
he has the hair.
The lights go up.
I was in good company:
the woman who didn't give me a job,
next to the trainer who thinks my dog has depression.
The man who wants the government
to stop killing wolves sits behind the painter
who pulls her feet to the seat like a child.
She's here each time I come,
trying, like me, to pay attention to genius.

LUCKY

She takes the corner leaning
like a biker, feels a wheel
not exactly skid, but nearly.
Her body, remembering,

does its electric-chair
clench, relaxes all at once.
She doesn't fall.
It was about this time last year

in about this spot she locked
and dropped. But ice
hasn't polished the road,
her wheels aren't slewing sideways,

she isn't sitting, staring at pavement,
linoleum-clean, unable to tell
a man on his knees her name.
The man took her to the hospital,

not talking as he drove,
staying in the car
while she waited in ER.
After someone glued

the tear in her scalp as if
she were a kindergarten project,
he was there still.
He took her home as quietly.

She couldn't say why

he went back to collect her bicycle,
stood in her yard aligning the wheels,
straightening the handlebars,
but wouldn't come in for a cup of tea.

THE PIANO TUNER

The Quasimodo of Hertfordshire
came once a year in his winged
leather overcoat, claws catching
in the latch of the black
wrought-iron gate my mother
washed back when outdoor
cleaning was normal.

Each visit he'd shed his coat
on the chair with short legs
and a broad lap too nice
for sitting in. I called him
Mr. Simmons to his face, only
stared at the crag of his back
when he couldn't see me looking.

Once when he was busy behind
his hump, manoeuvring levers and mutes,
I tried to heave his coat,
to hang it from the newel post
by the neck until it died.
It swooped me to the carpet,
making Quasimodo laugh.

I stayed low, watched
his ratcheting talons inside
the gutted piano, twisting pins.
He saw me looking, rose
to hover on the stool, flapped
his fingers, wings of music
wheeling above a sea of keys.

PARHELION

kicking snow on the way to the bus stop
it jangles as it skitters,
lit by star and street-lamp glitter.

Your scalp is tighter than a child's toque
by the time the bus is rattling
you through noisy air.

At work, everyone else is later than you.
You sit in your coat of dead-duck feathers
while your thighs thaw-burn back to warm.

You've had two meetings by the time
it's light, and people are saying
a cloudy sky would be a good thing

on a day like this,
but you're gawking out the window,
howling for a sun dog.

ST. MAARTEN

The man on the airport bus
takes me to a lady
who smells of sea grass.
She takes me to a room
with a bed, a table and a ceiling fan.

I tell her I can't afford
a room. That's why
I have a tent.
Oleanders and gum trees
will screen a small blue dome.

The room has a door that locks.
I give the lady francs.
I almost kiss her.
The room I stayed in
last night on Antigua

was free.
It had no lock.
It belonged to a man
who offered me a lift I took
because I'd walked all day.

He was proud of the house he'd built.
It still smelled of wet cement.
When I saw his wife's picture,
he told me she was away,
she wouldn't mind.

I said I did. I watched the handle
of the door to my room all night.
I left too early for him to take me
to the airport. I left a note
to thank him for the room.

I tell him I have a room.
He's stopped the car by the time
my foot is on the ground.

I run across sand to sea.
I stay in until I know I'll never
get cold, somersaulting, stretched
and weightless, letting water
hold me in a handstand.

A little girl is sitting by my towel.
She lives over there, she says.
She asks me where I'm from,
tells me my skin is broken
and will burn. When I've kept her

too long, I tell her to go home.
She says no one's there.
We stand with sand on our knees.
She holds out her hand for me to
pay her for the time she's sold me.

UNRAVELLED

By Friday nights, my brain was a net
of dripping dead fish.
Cycling home from work,
my thoughts were bitmapped,

the mistakes I'd made thudding
to the Tarmac. While emails subdivided,
I'd lick my eyeballs, stick them
to the television screen.

I know now how much my mind
can drink before the words drown.
Lying here unravelled, listening
to the shimmer of wind in aspens,

I wait for the crescendo to end.
It will take more than this week
of absence to wind my mind back in,
after a hundred and fifty days of unspooling,

sitting twisted in an adjustable chair,
my brilliant brief career. A Biro
was always best for spooling tape
back into a cassette, angled edges catching

in sprocket teeth. It was everywhere
in the eighties: shiny brown tape
tangled round lampposts, threaded
through dual-carriageway barriers.

I thought it came from the tapes
people chucked out their car windows
when Duran Duran snarled or snapped.
Carol, driving me through London,

said no. they were  the window.

I still have that tape, though I can't play it.
No one has cassette players any more.
The devil has found other ways
of getting messages to us.

WORK-LIFE BALANCE

Of course
I spend more hours
away from the office
than there.
I don't sleep under my desk

but balance it on my head,
carry it home,
lie in bed with it on top of me,
its feet on the floor like in old films.

AT WORK

I know more about
my colleagues than
I know about my friends.
Yesterday, a pregnancy
was delivered to my inbox
while I was labouring
under a deadline.
By the time I got round
to crafting congratulations,
it was a miscarriage.
I had to let go of the mouse
to wipe my eyes.
The week before, a cancer;
I was in the washroom for an hour.
I can't work this way.
I wish I could blast personal life
from my computer with
the air duster that shoots out
keyboard crumbs collecting
from too many lunches at my desk.
I daren't check the news today.
A strike-slip earthquake
has whip-cracked a tsunami
five thousand miles away
that will swipe me from my office,
send me home to check if my daughter
is really where her last text
said she was.

PETERHEAD, ABERDEENSHIRE

The sheets on the high bed
in the bay-windowed room
of the grey harling house
are briny-damp. Online it said
a sea view, but she hadn't expected
the tide to slosh under her bed.

In the morning, stretching her toes
to sand-grooved floorboards
she leaves the sheets at low tide
and goes to breakfast. The pinnied
man who checked her in
fumbles with a teapot, dripping

like wet hair on a beach towel
tea as orange as the marmalade
she can't eat. When she asks
for jam he brings honey,
tears in the corners of his mouth
are salted like the butter he didn't ask

if she wanted on cold white toast.
His wife, he says, would know about
jam, but she's gone back to London,
and she's the one who's Scottish,
who wanted to come home to a prison
and a thriving industry of seagulls.

He's grateful for the government
business and sorry about the jam.
He doesn't know how long
an English husband, wifeless,
can go on. Is she driving
all the way to London?

that don't allow passengers
in a little red fleet car.
Back in her room, she draws
brackish curtains to let in the soft
silhouette of an arctic tern.

She'll add a column to her claim
form for emotional expenditure;
she'll leave the bed unmade
to remind him to change
the sheets for the next person
who likes the idea of a sea view.

AT EACH EXHALE

PLAIN SAILING

sitting on the brim of the world.

It's an ill wind that makes her sick
to the gills. Munch told it how it was.
Only women die in his paintings.
She painted herself into a corner,
had to jump through Magritte's
trompe l'oeil window,
her final forgery. He called
her a plagiarist, incapable
of originality. His words as
hackneyed as the Hockneys
he doesn't know he's painting.

Maybe she'll learn to navigate
by the stars. In the meantime,
she's got both hands on deck,
trying not to go overboard,
trying to sleep a whole night through
without Fuseli's incubus hooked to her ribs.

He used to be the wind in her sails,
the port in her storm, not a cordillera
of waves salty as tears.
The thing about the horizon is,
she'll never get there.
She jumps in, treads water, fingers
shrivelling until her ring floats off.
All she really cares about
is what happened to the only woman
on Medusa's raft.

REGRET

her husband kneel to discuss
who will be Woody,

who will be Buzz.
His nephew folds beside him,
the shadows behind his knees

as deep as the crevices
she used to put shells in
for the sea to drown.

When Christmas comes,
she buys herself a puppy
and gives it to her husband.

She doesn't regret not having
children; she regrets
not wanting them.

PAST LIVES

He made me believe in past lives.
His tweeds, his waistcoat, creases
pointing to his polished shoes,
unexpected textures in the post-coital
nineteen-nineties.

His kisses missed me, landed
on my accent, the bonnet of the car
in which I drove him to the pub.
The nineteen-thirties were
his heyday.

I reckon he died a premature Nazi,
furious at missing the war.
Dead again by the time
the Berlin Wall got built.
Baby rage.

He kicked a car to death once
because he hated the way a man
at the marina where we worked
drove his yacht through the lock.
He told me

so many secrets when he was drunk,
I couldn't work out which side
he was on. Of course he said
he'd killed a man once.
It was his idea

to go Dutch on a B & B
far from our parents' houses.
My body knew best;
it wouldn't let him in.
I lay flat-flushed.

He tr...

...g ... each time
until the penny drops.
Reincarnation was made for men like him.

I CAN'T HEAR A THING YOU'RE SAYING

This big-box bar is trying to be dark,
though it's ten o'clock and light outside.
Low-wattage sun sparking through

not-quite-shut shutters makes me blink.
Ceiling fans spin, pretending it's hot.
It's not. It's as cold as any dwindling

Yukon August. I have come to this bar
so many times, trying to do what couples do.
Tonight we are on stools,

in the section that I hate the most.
I can't talk in blaring lines,
just quiet squares and circles.

Tonight I can't talk at all in this factory
of racket, being born with a blunt voice,
dull ears. If I can hear you, I don't

want to because you must be shouting.
I watch a guy by the bar at artless ease
in a ball cap, nothing to do but chew gum

and pull at his T-shirt. I want to sketch
the sphere of his abundant midriff.
I'm grateful no one smokes in bars

any more, that these fancy ceiling tiles
are white, but tomorrow, when I can hear
myself speak, I'll tell you I'm never

coming here again. Get some other
mug to drive you. I'm going to stay
at home and drink alone.

FORTY

Your browser history deleted our history
with a one-fingered click
when I turned forty
and you turned to pornography,
putting in the Macintosh a stain
too deep for me to get out.
As I unzip your hockey bag,
you say men and women are different.
I screw up glabrous and blonde pages
to set the wood stove,
staples burning in chemical flames.

MARRIAGE

He prefers, when the telephone rings,
to let it finish.
He's never been one to interrupt.
She says it's rude to listen
to people leaving messages.

When they walk down the street,
he holds to his ear the tape measure
he keeps in his pocket,
talks loudly of being on a train.
She always laughs.

She wonders where the first two
syllables of telephone have gone,
the apostrophe. There's a heap
of letters and punctuation marks somewhere,
mixed in with fountain pens
and sanitary-napkin belts.

No one says aeroplane or omnibus
any more, he says. The end of
pianoforte fell off, not the front.
And it should be tele, she says, not telly.

You didn't used to be able, he says,
to buy a telephone with a dial any more
and now they're everywhere.
Never Bakelite, she says.
They look like it, but as soon
as you pick them up, you know:
they're too light.
Weight is the sixth sense, she says.
No one ever talks about that.

SCIENTIST

when you stop abruptly
before a bough across our path
slung with a slack rope of snow,
a loop impossibly air-held,
a single winter garland.

You twist a wrist to flick a pole
to break it. I shout, don't!
meaning many things.
You say you need to see what
holds it there. I say seeing means
it won't be there any more.

While you talk of riming
and colliding crystals, I recall
my mother's oldest friend
telling me her husband
was the sort to pause
to gaze at dew drops,

how, if I were lucky,
I'd meet a man like him.
Now you're saying that snowflakes,
when they reach the ground,
take up ten times
more space than rain.

AT SEA

The ebb and flow
of your breath
is the calm gush and suck
of sea on a stony beach.
At each exhale,
my thumbnail slides
and scores the sheet,
rasps soft cotton,
sounding in the trough
of sleep like the creak
of the teak that took me
trans-Atlantic.

Twenty years ago
I hitched a ride
on the *Lady Francesca*
with a jolly crew
who threw me
in the bosun's chair,
swung me out over
sea as deep and dark
as sky at night,
my feet garnishing
a shark's dinner plate.

RECOVERY POINT

to soothe the water, taste
the salt to preserve my desire
for the world. I'll close my eyes
to listen to the stroke and slap
of swell that never stills.

You don't need a coast.
You don't have to feel
for the edge to work out
where you are.
We live where our plates
tessellate, a united state.

I'm waiting for my baggage
before I see you tilt across
the concourse in that green
coat you've had for years,
too thick for me to feel
your shoulder blades.

I kiss the cumin
and coriander in your hair,
ginger on your lips.
As you drive me home
and talk, I'm guessing
saag paneer.

TOUCHING MY HUSBAND

She passes me. She passes him.
She trips. Her long hair jolts.
He reaches to catch her.
She stretches to be caught.
They lock wrists
in a monkey grip.
I watch them look.

Wrists are where to run the tap
to cool the blood, where
to take the pulse
or kiss.

We've been together years
yet never bound ourselves
together with such strong rope as this.

This is the moment my husband
starts forgetting me,
a wife from a past life
he doesn't believe in.

VANCOUVER HEART

Thi

...ay.

I remembered salt water,
forgot about tides.

I press my palm to the heartless
side of your ribcage,
slide back to the heartful.
Yesterday at Science World
we stared at a heart in a box,

felted, grey and frayed,
next to a bloodless half-capped brain,
beside amphibious lungs.
You laid your palm on a machine
that made your heartbeat public.

You breathed fast to drum your blood.
When it was my turn, I breathed
deep to slow my heartbeat down,
so everyone would know
how calm I was.

NOBODY ELSE DIES

WALKING IN THE ENGLISH COUNTRYSIDE ON A SUNNY DAY

ᴏꜰ a cow ꜰrom braɪn to arse.

These Friesians aren't edible;
they're milk machines.
They're the glass and a half
in my daily Cadbury's.

Herbivores work hard
to digest perennial meals,
breeding bacteria
to decompose cellulose.

Despite the easy heat,
my jaws are clamped
as I watch the rumination.
Clenched all night, the dentist says.

She's ordered me a mouthguard
to stop my bovine molar grinding,
my perpetual reflex to feed.
It's easier for carnivores.

Their stomachs come
with a set of enzymes.
Why don't we give stomachs the
significance we give hearts?

71

Let's talk of the stomach
of the matter, of a woman after our
own stomach, of abstinence making
the stomach grow emptier.

I, omnivore, lean on the gate
and watch the breeze wipe its hand
on the grass, observing that cows
are the shape of the United States.

BIOLOGY LESSON

Everything killed something

else in order to survive.
I called out that I didn't;
I was a herbivore.
He told me I'd get ill;

I wasn't a cow or a rabbit.
The class thought that was funny.
I sketched a rabbit on the cover
of my exercise book.

I had a rabbit at home
with a tumour on his spine.
I was keeping him alive.
On Sunday, my mother made me

help her dig the garden.
She sat back on the heels
of her rubber boots, muddying
the backside of her old blue trousers.

She said, last week I stuck a fork
into the soil and heard a scream.
She'd stabbed a frog.
She definitely heard it scream.

I was the first person she'd told.
She'd put the body in the compost.
She wished now she'd buried it
where the daffodils grew.

We watched a mosquito bite
her forearm, blood ballooning
in its abdomen. It looked too heavy
to fly, but it reached the raspberries.

If my mother had squashed it, her
own blood would have smeared her skin.
She started digging with the fork,
but I dug with blunt fingers.

I was the heroine in a film, mud-smeared
face, long black hair flowing,
a silhouette against a thunderous sky,
shouting, nobody else dies here!

WHITE DOG

Walk to Chur...

...walk across
the Arabian Sea to Haji Ali tomb
because the causeway was too crowded.

Don't worry that you're the only
woman in the carriage. Watch people
living beside the railway tracks, drying
their bright sheets on dusty bushes.
Get off at Malad Station.
Go up the steps past the five-year-old
girl sitting cross-legged with a baby
in her lap. Fold the girl's fingers
over the bills. You can wonder
whether she belongs to the beggar
mafia for the rest of your life.

Turn left out of the station. Turn
right at the end of the road.
You're in Natraj Market.
You won't see many Europeans,
unlike in the bar of the Taj Hotel.
Look for a store selling toffees
to take home for presents.
There are, as usual, dogs.
One dog, white,
is curled up in the heat
while others lie outstretched,
looking dead. You've learnt
they are just practising.

The white dog is shaking.
Look for food to give her.
See bananas. Pakora,
or something like it.
Don't think water might be best.
You have some in your bag.
Don't touch her.
Be afraid of catching a disease.
Buy nothing.
Keep walking. Know
you are the reason
there is no hope in the world.

KEEPING WARM IN ANTARCTICA

Yes, fairies live at the South Pole,
softly plucking each other's breasts,
cooing sorry when it hurts,
knitting sweaters from snowflakes
to stay warm until the down grows back.

Men bounce and dash on snowmobiles,
smash the ice sealed over
stillness, and park next to prey
who don't bother flying away.
They stuff fistfuls of fairies into sacks,
tip them out on a factory floor.
They hang them by the wisps
of their ankles, dunk them
in electrified baths, cut
their throats, drop their bodies
in scalding water, because that's
how to make feathers pop out easily.

YEAR OF THE SHEEP

Our ancestors were cleared
to the cliffs in the year of the sheep,
children and livestock rock-tethered
against the wind that blew boats
to New Caledonia.

Not everyone sailed.
Some clung to the crags
while sheep sheared Scotland bare,
making way for attrition
by Munro-baggers.

You and I overshot our families
by three thousand miles
and two hundred years when
we ran aground in the Yukon,
high-jumping the sixtieth parallel.

A new friend took you up
ungrazed hills for days
with guns, brought you back
with sacks of bone and muscle.
As his truck triumphed off,

you stood in the driveway,
threw up and stayed outside
to watch your vomit melt
the snow. A month shy of
Guy Fawkes Night, you cut

a bonfire out the back, a pyre
to roast your vengeance meat.
I brought you a mug of tea, flipped
the memory card into black flames
after I saw pictures of you,

knees astride

but had slaughtered horned Cernunnos,
the Celtic god of life.

RED CANOE

A red canoe complements
the deep green summer
that seduces me, kneeling
as I scoop and spoon

along a liquid highway.
Forests pool like oceans
in flat valleys that would
drown me if I fell in.

I miss the low damp Celtic sky
of home just once during
large days of northern sun.
Camping in a wild rose garden,

I stand, arms raised to entice
an absent rain. Along a fire
break, I find a moose's rack
embracing a yellow-eyed crocus.

I circle, collecting stones
to arrange an atheist's shrine.
No Romans ever levelled,
no cartwheels ever rutted

this arid track. It was
hacked by chainsaws
along a trail already trodden.
I'm from a conquered country,

SALT FLATS

A sequined blackbird lets us pass,
chucking lumps of mudded grass,
busy tugging bugs. You're taking me

and a shouldered telescope
to a secret you can't keep, screened
by tidy spruce and cluttered aspen.

You come here each annual meadow
greening, tramping a leaf-and-needle drop
that takes two decades to rot.

There. A low blue lake,
not yet unplugged by summer.
A saucer of salt-rimmed margarita water

you say you've never tasted. I finger-tip
lick it, not even brackish, nearly sweet,
as you focus on redpolls in the sand.

Sea asparagus veins the lens
as I twist to see hill-snow whiter
than the clouds above.

At last, the spring heat stills me.
Sitting on our coats, we're periscoped
by a hummocked ground squirrel.

I swing the squatted lens to count dotted
whisker roots, and one almond eye.
You should not have shared this

secret salt pool. I hiss the squirrel
back into its hole. I clap to slap
the redpolls against the sky.

FISH LAKE RIDGE

W̶̶̶̶̶̶̶̶̶̶̶̶̶ ̶̶̶̶̶ ̶̶̶̶ and fell the bull.

On Fish Lake ridge, this
other peoples' land, I stand
on silver granite dry with lichen.
Stepping to the liquid view,
I startle a ptarmigan, rising low
to cling to camouflage. Liver
of vitamin A, breast of vitamin B.
I know what can be done
with a gun and guts.

No ancestors watch over me.
I have no descendants to guard.
My native land is a high street
of Ford Fiestas parked
outside a Tudor-fronted Tesco
Metro selling tuna sandwiches.
My territory is bounded by
a fence my father creosotes
every second summer.

THE NAMES OF THINGS

How many of us look and listen
as people tell us the names of
natural things, wanting to know.
You remember this purple and yellow
now at your feet is prairie crocus.
Pinker purple along July highways
is fireweed, that's easy.
You recognize the chickadee-dee-dee's
call (or it might be the song). You've
learnt that the bird that bullets into woods
as you cycle is an American Robin,
flying low to find berries but not worms,
not this far north, where soil is undigested.
Yet you never can remember the difference
between a black spruce and a white, however
often you're told white has longer needles.
You'd think living among millions of them,
eating their spring tips, carrying that cat-pee
smell into your house each Christmas,
you'd know it, as parents know twins.
You've been told to look at the ground:
if it's wet it's black and if it's dry it's
white, but in spring and autumn all the earth
is drenched and in winter there's the snow.
Sometimes you know willows from alders,
yet never have you recalled
a mushroom's name the next day.
It's not lack of interest,
it's just there's never time to go over
what you're told, too many other things to do.
On Sunday, you will walk this way
again, you'll bring a guidebook,
notebook and camera.

STONE

Each time I ran my loop in Scotland,
I'd see the stone spilled by a
broadening beech tree

settling beside a drystone wall.
Between pignut and dandelion,
pale when it hadn't rained,

it marked the place I'd stop,
even if my shoelaces weren't untied,
where the lane, rising to a falling wall,

was proof of man-made perfection,
beside a stand of rangy pines,
soft squares of brown and green

pinned to the red-bridged Forth beyond.
Often, when I was sure I was unwatched,
I stroked the moss cushioning the road.

In the unbound, endless Yukon,
I don't listen for human-nature harmonies.
Running, I am a breathing space

between millions of wood- and water-miles.
Head above the treeline for a clear view,
I'm grateful for a road through all this spruce.

I try not to be nostalgic for a place
I chose to leave for a place unbroken.

I shouldn't really care if anyone
ever put back that stone.

EARTH CRACK

shouldering into the lake.
Or it could be the strain
of all our freight upon this Earth:

books we own instead of borrow,
clothes we replace instead of mend,
boats and canoes we keep

for a quarter of summer
under tarps low with snow,
cars and trucks we euthanize.

Redistributing the weight
might give us a chance,
if shipping wasn't so pricey

and the Red Cross offered
pick-ups here. What if the dotted line
of the Arctic Circle just above me

on the map is a perforation?
What if the piece of the world
I'm on tears off?

CAT AND MOUSE

The charity tin-shaker has a nice smile,
but I'm too busy leading myself out
of temptation on Main Street
to walk his way, until I spot
the pink ribbon on his can.

Got a minute for cancer research?
A donation?
A bequest is best.

How many mouse mutations
to the pound, I want to know.
How many monkey mammaries
would a monthly debit fund?
How many dog disembowelments
is each donation worth?

His face is unwritten,
like the cheque
that will stay in my purse.
He's *never been asked that before.*
He doesn't tell me about
his sister/mother/girlfriend like he should,
or remind me of my best friend's
reconstructed breasts.

I give him my authentic smile.
I even say I'm sorry
because he's not the one
who stole Tabitha
when I was eight.
He doesn't give cats
cancer or AIDS,
doesn't test medicines
for headaches they
only get when holes
are drilled into their skulls.

TEN THOUSAND TREES

...a car ...ing when a journey takes too long.

Blue sky would have made better photographs.
Spring would have made good television: ash twigs
hoofed with sticky buds. A soggy autumn breeze
might have blown more activists into the branches

to snag like plastic bags. Yet seven thousand of us
came to stand and march if not to climb. The blunt light
of winter hammered high figures into silhouettes,
narrowing drainpipe jeans, as the protesters rose

to their willow twigloos, not touching ground for days.
A decade later, when we toured England to say goodbye,
the sky was blue. We pretended to forget we'd vowed
never to use the road that uprooted ten thousand trees.

Sliding between the gaudy fields, I looked up at Middle Oak,
the only tree the protest saved, too thick with glossy leaves
for us to see if plastic bags were caught within its branches.
I thought of Newbury today because a clearcut caught me out,

a scalp shaved to the Yukon River since I last drove this way,
preparation for the operation to cut a commute from fourteen
minutes to nine. I hope the spruce sap buggered up the machinery.
But wilderness creep has got to me. There's so much space

in Canada; so many bloody trees, scrawny as schoolboy legs
too thin to hold up socks. I didn't know the flash
of a forest gash could mesmerize, that there could even be a lust
to witnessing the first road ever forced on feral land.

THE FLEECE ERA

it in his truck full of wood,
and she told his tanned hands
on the wheel she'd just found
her way out of the biggest forest
she'd ever almost got lost in.
He said, look around,
you're not out yet.
She said, what's it like living
in a forest as big as a country?
He said, it's hard to believe but
there are lands here where
the forest doesn't grow, cities
where burning wood is not allowed.
Big deal, he said, we can make
sweaters out of plastic pop
bottles, yet there are places
where it's illegal to hang your
washing out to dry, places
where children never get the tips
of their noses nubbed
by the smell of photosynthesis
as they pull a sun-dried T-shirt
down over their heads.

THIS IS THE HOUSE

This is the house where the dog
clambers off the couch

to cool on the carpet.
This is the town where the people

idle their car engines year-round.
This is the land where winter

is feeling its age.
This is the planet that is sunlit,

overheating.
This is the land that burns coal

to keep the people warm.
This is the town that sets fire

to its garbage.
This is the creek that is melting,

flooding.
These are the aspens marooned

like abandoned punting poles,
as if the leisured classes were

the first to flee.
This is the dog shaking after

cooling off in the creek,
droplets drying before they reach the grass.

MOUNTAIN TIME

The p̶a̶r̶k̶i̶n̶g̶ ...

from asphalt built for axles.

A woman in an SUV,
chatting to her friend,
is driving straight at me,
though there's everywhere
else to go. I fail at eye contact,
recalibrate my direction.
I'm not annoyed
– I'm a bad driver too –
but the convergence is curious,
our intersection in emptiness.

Aiming for Succulent Samosas,
I pass gulls on soggy grass,
a shortcut straight into
the path of the only
other vehicle I've seen.
I magnetize it to a stop
to let me cross,
run and raise a hand
to apologize for my lack
of urban timing.

But it's not that I've been
on mountain time too long:
the pavement is as bare
as wet grey sky.
The mall lacks lines
to help us hear
the rhythm of the road.
We need painted staves
if we are to keep
to the beat of infrastructure.

EDIPHILE

is a Guggenheim to me.
I'm climbing the clay,
looking for the steel
that holds up the clouds.

LANDOWNER

It takes eighty years
of coming down the same
broad staircase to notice
at the ninth stair he can see
all his favourite possessions:
the van Dyck on his mother's side,
Handel's harpsichord,
the Louis XVI table on which
he has eaten, slept, loved.

Yet there is no point
from which he can see all his land,
his eighty thousand acres.
He hires a helicopter
but it can't fly high enough
to fit each crooked burn and crag,
each ben and sheltered loch,
each crease and fold,
into one gaze.
If he could stretch it out,
pull it taut, his land would cover
all of Britain, hang off the sides
like a tablecloth.

NEO-COLONIALIST

It was a lark at first to immigrate:
homeless, jobless, carless, carefree.
Until we had to spend the money
we made on the house.
We'd never experienced grocery store
trauma before. We had to shop at Walmart
and save Canadian Tire money.

At last we listened to the rumour of the north.
Now, our government jobs keep *Canis lupus*
from the door and our coats lined,
the Subaru fuelled and the skis waxed.
We love the smell of spruce sap
in the morning.

Canada is the perfect place to come to
now that England is full up.
The towns are ugly, but
there's space for everyone
in this megaland. We might go
country residential next year.
Clear some trees so we can see the
mountains but not the neighbours.

YOU WERE PROBABLY GENETICALLY PROGRAMMED

to leave your parents, country,
sit for hours on buses, trains,
sleep on railway platforms, in cemeteries,
on a beach when you could find one,
once in a truck driver's cab.

Everything you needed was in a backpack
you'd keep forever as a memento,
hang on the wall until you slung
it on a landfill heap greased
by takeout packaging, oil.

You could have used the fabric
for a collage, the way you cut up
all your paintings after college.
You used to be so creative.
You have no urge to travel any more,

the only thing that makes you believe
you've changed. It's true you live
abroad now and life's a journey anyhow.
Your contentment to stay in one place
reminds you of spring lambs.

Watching them jump and twist,
you used to want one as a pet. By late
summer they'd always stop, stand
cropping grass beside their placid mothers,
wool as grubby as your New Zealand socks.

You couldn't tell the difference
between lambs and mothers
when they were taken away
in trucks to be stunned and sliced,
the husks of that expended energy

EARTH TWIN

The cat drinks from the sink,
an onion skin floats to the floor,
a scientist on the radio says
we are always searching for other
planets that can support human life.
The onion skin splinters as I pick it up.
If anyone ever asks whether I believe
in life on other planets, I say yes
right away. I don't need to think
about it like I do with most questions.
The scientist says we're a universe
in a multiverse; I consider an endless
poem. His point, he tells us,
as I crane the cat to the floor, is
that there might be planets even more
suitable for human life than ours.
I use the dishcloth to wipe slivers
of onion skin from the floor. It takes
a day or so for me to comprehend
he was talking about Heaven.

ACKNOWLEDGEMENTS

also appeared in *Walk Mysey Home* (Caitlin Press) and on a table at Baked Café, Whitehorse.

I have had much help with writing the poems in this book. I am grateful to my editor, Barry Dempster, for his kindness and for seeing what I didn't know was there, and to Karen Connelly, my mentor at the Humber School for Writers, who was generous with her insights and encouragement.

The support I have received since moving to Yukon has been a joy. Thank you to the talented and inspiring Whitehorse writing community, particularly Lily Gontard, Jamella Hagen, kjmunro, Clea Roberts and Patricia Robertson. And thank you to the Government of Yukon for granting me an Advanced Artist Award.

It isn't only the writing support that matters. My friends in England and Scotland sustain me always: Kate Chalk, Claire Hider, Kim Mason and Jordan Pullicino. As do my strong and loving parents, John and Patricia Lilley, and my gifted siblings – Matthew, Rebecca, Lucy and Melissa – and their families.

I owe the most, of course, to Glenn, my husband, without whom I would not have stood on as many mountains and seen as many panoramas and possibilities.

JOANNA LILLEY was born in Newmarket, Suffolk, and lived in England, Wales and Scotland before moving to Whitehorse, Yukon, in 2006. *The Fleece Era* is her first book.